DATE DUE

MAY 2 8 1993			
NOV 1 9 2009			
	261-2500		Printed in USA

Art for City Children

Norman Krinsky

Art" for City Children

VNR VAN NOSTRAND REINHOLD COMPANY

NEW YORK   CINCINNATI   TORONTO   LONDON   MELBOURNE

Also by the author (with Bill Berry):
Paper Construction for Children

Van Nostrand Reinhold Company Regional Offices:
New York Cincinnati Chicago Millbrae Dallas

Van Nostrand Reinhold Company Foreign Offices:
London Toroton Melbourne

Designed by Rosa Delia Vasquez

Printed by Halliday Lithograph Corporation
Bound by William Marley Company

Published by Van Nostrand Reinhold Company
450 West 33rd Street, New York, N.Y. 10001

Published simultaneously in Canada by
D. Van Nostrand Company (Canada), Ltd.

16 15 14 13 12 11 10 9 8 7 6 5 4 3 2 1

Contents

WHAT THIS BOOK IS ABOUT

The children who made the pictures in this book are very much like you and your friends. They live in a big city and do many of the things you do. They live in apartments which are sometimes too small and they go to schools which are overcrowded and never have enough desks or books or pencils or anything. After school, they play with their friends in playgrounds or parks or in the street. When they go home they like to watch television. Some of them are very good at their studies and others are not good at all. But one subject they are all good at and all of them enjoy is art. One reason why art is everybody's favorite subject is because it is fun. It is also easy. Everybody is good at it because there are no rules about how a picture is supposed to look. The only test of whether a picture is good or not is if you like it.

Besides being fun, art is a good way to learn about many things and to remember experiences that you've enjoyed. It is a good way to express your feelings and to tell stories. It is one of the oldest forms of communication. It is older than writing. The first writing was really pictures and our own alphabet is derived from these pictures. Art is a good way to share what you know with others and to make gifts that are not like anybody else's. It is something you can do all by yourself or together with your friends. When you look through the pictures in this book, you will see some of the things other children have done in their art classes and at home, and get some ideas for what you can do.

Although you have probably been drawing pictures ever since you were old enough to hold a pencil, in this book you will find some new things to try. You will use pencils and other things that are already familiar to you and some things you may never have thought of using. You will find directions, and see pictures made by children who have followed these directions.

This book is about drawing, printing, painting, and making sculpture with Plasticine and papier maché and about the children who have had fun doing these things. We think you will too!

Drawing

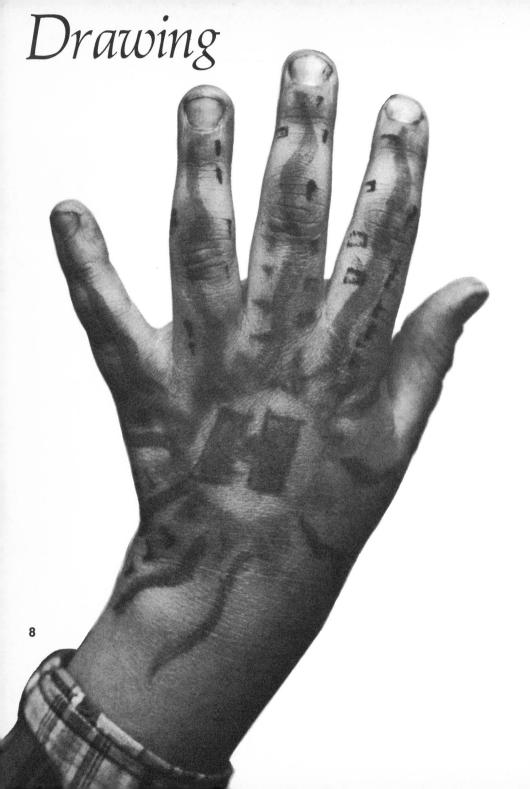

Although you may not remember it, you drew pictures before you learned to write, and even now you probably draw a lot more than you realize. Just look quickly through your notebooks and see how many pages are filled with drawings.

Drawing is basic to all the other kinds of art, and an artist must learn to draw before he does anything else. Drawing is also the simplest art to start with — all you need is something to draw with and something to draw on. You could use chalk on the sidewalk or pencil on paper.

Blocking In

Drawing is fun and drawing is easy, but drawing can also be frustrating if your picture never comes out the way you want it to. Sometimes this is because the picture you draw is not quite like the picture in your imagination. There is a very simple way of starting that will help you to draw pictures that look more like the thing you want to draw. It is called blocking in.

Suppose you decide that you want to draw an animal — a tiger, for instance. Although you think you know exactly what a tiger looks like, chances are that if you start to draw it from your imagination it will not come out looking just right. So, unless you can spend a lot of time in the zoo, it is a good idea to find a picture of a tiger in a book or magazine and use it as a model. Look at the picture carefully. Is the tiger sitting, standing, or running? How large are you going to make him on your paper and where are you going to place him? Now you can start blocking in:

1. Starting with the head, draw a box that is about the size and shape of the tiger's head you want to draw. This first box is very important because it determines the size of the head in relationship to the body. If it is half as big as the head in the picture, remember to make the neck and body of the tiger half as big. If it is twice as big, make the rest of the tiger twice as big too. Also, if you don't place the head right on the paper, you might not have room for the rest of the body.

2. Now draw boxes for the neck, body, and legs of the tiger. If you study the picture of the blocked-in tiger on this page, you will notice that the boxes lead into each other, usually from the corner. This gives a flow to the drawing and helps you place every part in its proper position.

3. When you have blocked in the whole figure, study the original picture again and use this to help place the details — the eyes, ears, tail, feet, and stripes of the tiger.

Once you know how to block in a picture, you can draw anything — even something as different from a tiger as a freight ship. Just follow the same steps as before:

Tiger / Gail age 9 / Crayon drawing on 12x18 manila paper

1. Find a picture that you like and study it carefully.

2. Make a line near the bottom of your paper to indicate the water.

3. Block in the hull by drawing a long rectangle. This will determine the size of your ship.

4. Now you can draw in all the other parts of the ship, and then use your imagination to surround the ship with fish, submarines, deep-sea divers, or anything else you can think of.

You will find that if you practice blocking in you will improve your drawings and soon you will be able to draw anything. The most difficult subjects will become easy for you.

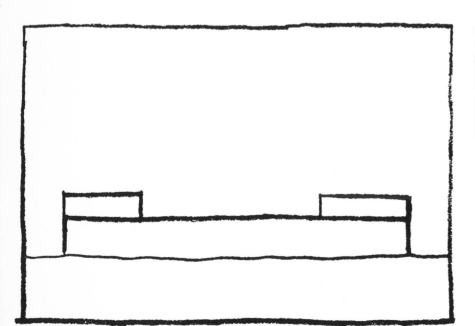

Freighter / Jerome
age 11 / Crayon on
12x18 manila paper

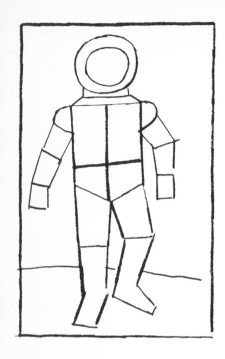

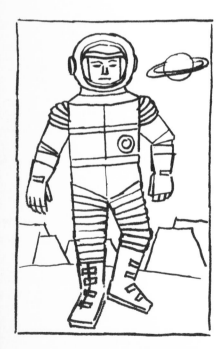

Astronaut in space / Ginella age 10 / Crayon on 12x18 manila paper

Deep-sea diver / Medin age 9 / Crayon on 12x18 manila paper

What You Will Need

When you are just beginning to draw, it doesn't matter what tools you use. Probably you have been using a pencil, and this is one of the best tools for making small, detailed drawings. You can get pencils easily, and you can erase what you don't like. Different tools are good for different things. When you want to work on larger pieces of paper and use color it is easier and more fun to use crayons and colored chalks (also known as pastels).

Crayons are one of the most inexpensive and easily available drawing materials. They come in every color imaginable. Although you can use crayons just like all the other drawing tools you have worked with, there are special things that you can do with crayons that you can't do with anything else.

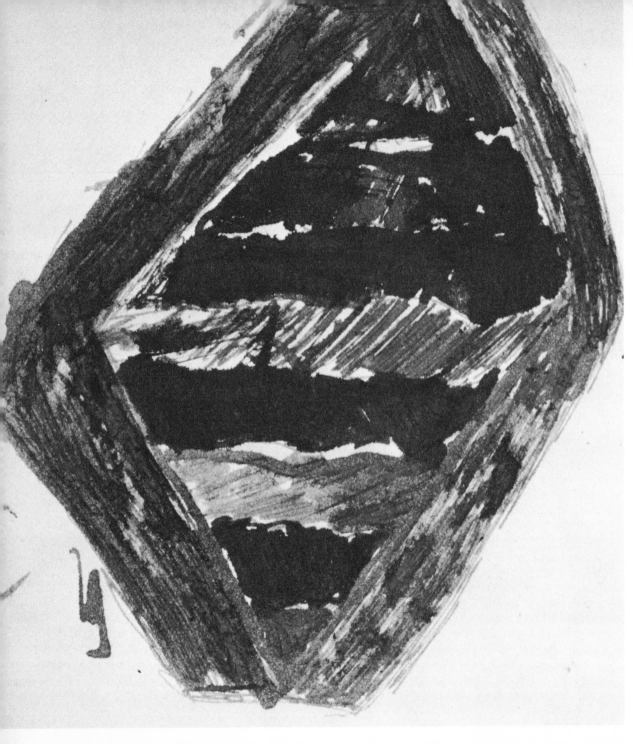

Flowers / Ellen age 11 / Pen and brush and colored inks white drawing paper.

Design/George age 9/colored ink drawing done with a wood stick.

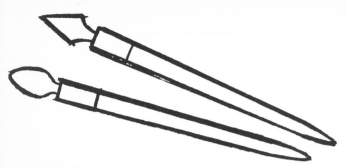

Scratch Drawings

One of the most interesting things that you can do with crayons is to make a scratch drawing. You do this by covering your paper with a thick layer of crayon. You can use any color or combination of colors, except black. Then cover the crayon color with black crayon until you do not see the color underneath. Using a sharp tool, such as a nail, paper clip, or old ball-point pen, make a design or drawing by scratching away the black. You can also use black india ink instead of the black crayon. It works the same way.

These drawings work better when they are not too large, because it takes a long time to cover the paper with layers of crayon and because the fine lines made by scratching will be lost on a very large surface.

Always cover your working space and the floor around you with newspapers, because doing scratch drawings gets very messy.

If you find that you like doing these drawings, you can get a product called scratch board. One side is coated with a white clay-like substance which you cover with india ink. Then you scratch the black surface with special points that fit in a pen holder. There are many different shapes of points so you can make many different kinds of lines. But you only need a few to get a lot of interesting effects.

Abstract design / Lorenzo age 12 / scratch drawing with india ink over crayon

Pirate ship / Benjamin age 12 / Crayon scratch drawing on 9x12 oak tag

Heart / Armeta age 11 / Crayon scratch drawing

House in a storm / Jill age 12 / Scratch drawing india ink over crayon on 6x9 heavy paper.

Flag / Patricia age 10 / 5x8 commercial scratchboard

Football player / Daniel age 11 / 5x8 commercial scratchboard

25

Crayon Resist

Have you ever heard of crayon resist? Crayons are made of wax, which means that they are waterproof (they resist water). If you get some poster paint, which is a paint made with water, you can make a crayon-resist picture. Here's how. First make a design or drawing with crayons. Then thin some black poster paint with water. Do this by putting a little poster paint in an empty glass or milk carton with the top cut off, and then add water. Don't put the water into the paint jar. Now, using a wide brush, go over the crayon drawing with paint. You will see that the paint will not cover the drawing but will crawl to the edges. This will make a very beautiful design, and your picture will glisten from the paint. Remember to let it dry before you pick up your picture. By experimenting with different colors you can make many unusual pictures in this way.

Sun/ Betty age 7/ Print made from crayon resist drawing

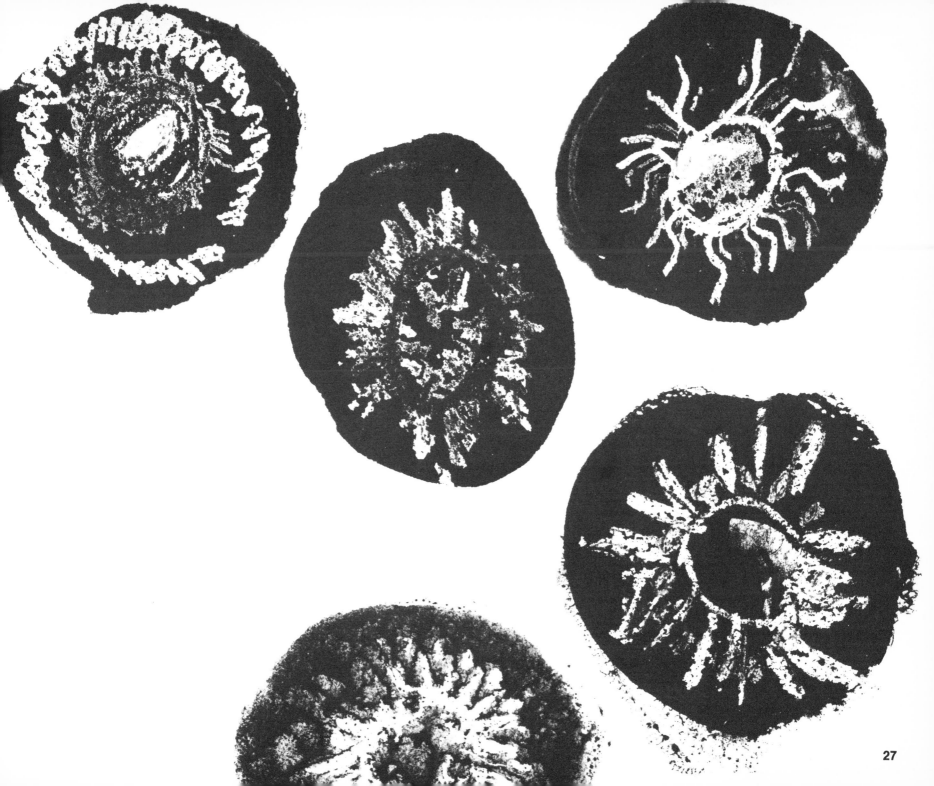

Colored Chalks

You can make a completely different kind of color picture when you use colored chalks, or pastels. Pastel colors are more brilliant than those you get from crayons, and the colors can be mixed together on paper to make new colors. You should work on fairly large pieces of paper. When the picture is finished, spray it with a fixative or clear varnish to keep it from smudging. Because the chalks raise quite a bit of dust when you work with them, you should keep your working space covered and wear a smock, or old clothes. It is also best to keep a window open, especially when you spray the fixative.

Flower and bird / Gladys age 12 / Colored chalks on 40x48 paper

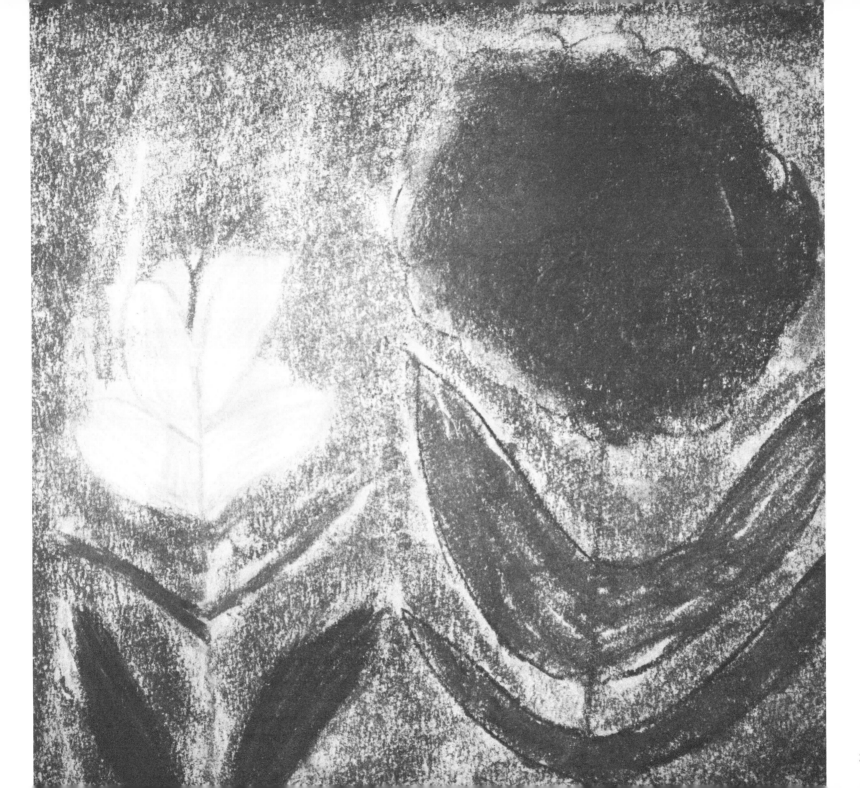

Batman/ George age 9/ Colored chalks on 24 x 36 brown drawing paper

Batman and Robin / Felix age 9 / Colored chalks on 24x36 brown wrapping paper

Drawing Collage

The only tools you need to make a drawing collage are paste, scissors, paper and something to draw with. The drawings can be done with pencil, pen, crayons or felt tipped markers. It is an easy and interesting way to make a large picture of a complicated subject. For example: suppose you wanted to make a picture of a city. There are so many things in a city—buildings, cars, trees, and people, that you might think it a difficult picture to do. But if you wanted to draw just a building or a car you would find it easy.

In a drawing collage you draw everything you want to be in your city on separate small pieces of paper. Then cut out the shapes and arrange and paste them on a large sheet of paper.

One of the many nice things about this kind of collage is that you can make changes by simply pasting over what you don't like. You can paste on colored construction paper, instead of coloring things yourself. You can also paste on objects to add texture.

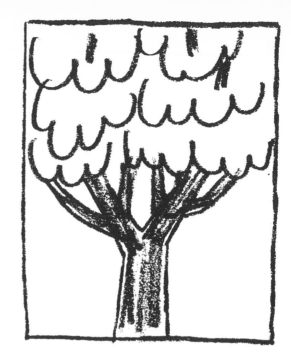

Street scene/Marianne age 7/crayon drawings, cut out and made into a collage.

Boy in snow storm/ Kathy age 7/ Cut-outs pasted on construction paper 12 x 18

Clown / Connie age 11 / tissue paper and paint

Other Materials

Charcoal is also fun to draw with, even if it is a little messy, like pastels. Remember to spray charcoal pictures with fixative, too.

Felt-tipped pens come in many colors. They glide over the paper so smoothly that it is fun to draw when you have one in your hand.

Once you have tried all these tools, you will find for yourself which ones you like best, and which help you to make the best drawings.

By dividing your paper into boxes, it becomes easy to tell a story.

Spring and summer trees/ Helen age 12/ Colored felt-tip markers

Printing

If printing had not been invented, you would not be in school today. For a long time, only a very few people knew how to read or write. When somebody drew something or wrote something, there was only one of it, and so only a few people could see the picture or learn to read. With the invention of the printing press, many copies could be made of the same drawing or writing.

You can use printing in many different ways and you will be surprised at how easy it really is. You can make copies of your own pictures and use them for birthday or Christmas cards and other gifts. You can print on almost any kind of paper — the children whose work is shown in this book used white drawing paper, manila paper, and rice paper. You can try printing on anything, even on cloth.

What You Will Need

In order to print, you will need ink and a rubber printing roller. There are two kinds of ink you can use, one made with water and one made with oil. The water-base ink is easier to clean up because you can use water, but it is slower to dry. The oil-base ink dries faster, but you need turpentine to clean up. Both come in tubes much like toothpaste and are available in many colors. If you can't get ink and a roller, or want to try something different, you can also use poster paints and apply them with a brush.

"Q" / Helen age 10 / Detail of cardboard print

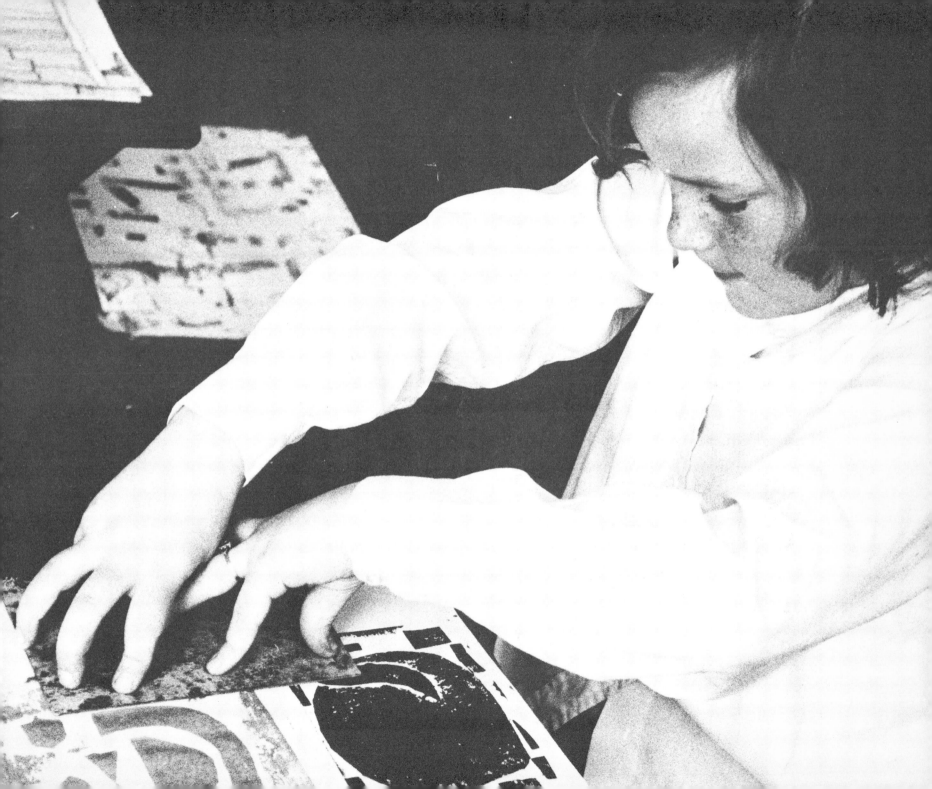

Printing With Cardboard

Now you are ready to make your printing blocks. The simplest way to print is with cardboard. The kind of cardboard that comes in shirts is just the right kind because it is thin enough to cut with scissors. You start by drawing simple shapes, like circles, squares, diamonds, or stars on the cardboard. If you make letters, remember that they have to be glued on backwards to come out right when printed. You now have a printing block and can start to make prints. Here's how:

1. First squeeze out some ink on a piece of heavy cardboard or on kitchen waxed paper. If you use waxed paper, tape it down so it doesn't slide around. Don't use too much ink to start.

2. Coat your roller with the ink by rolling it over the ink several times until it is completely and evenly covered. If you need a little more ink, squeeze it out and roll your roller over it again.

3. Now cover your printing block completely with ink by rolling the roller over it several times. Only the shapes you pasted down will have ink on them — not the piece of cardboard to which you pasted them.

4. Now you are ready to print. Place your paper carefully on the printing block and, using the back of a spoon, rub the paper. Make several prints to learn just how much pressure and rubbing produce the best results.

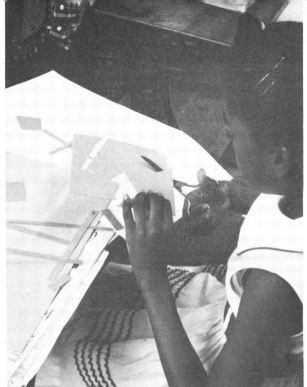

Print / Peter age 12 / water ink and cardboard letters printed on white paper

Other Things To Print With

Don't forget about obvious things to print with, like your hands and fingers. By simply dipping them in ink and then pressing them to the paper you can make interesting designs and patterns. Try combining fingerprints with the design made by your printing block. Also try printing the same design over and over again in different colors.

If you look at the pictures of the prints made by the children in this book, you will be able to get many ideas for your own printing. The more you do it, the more ideas will come to you.

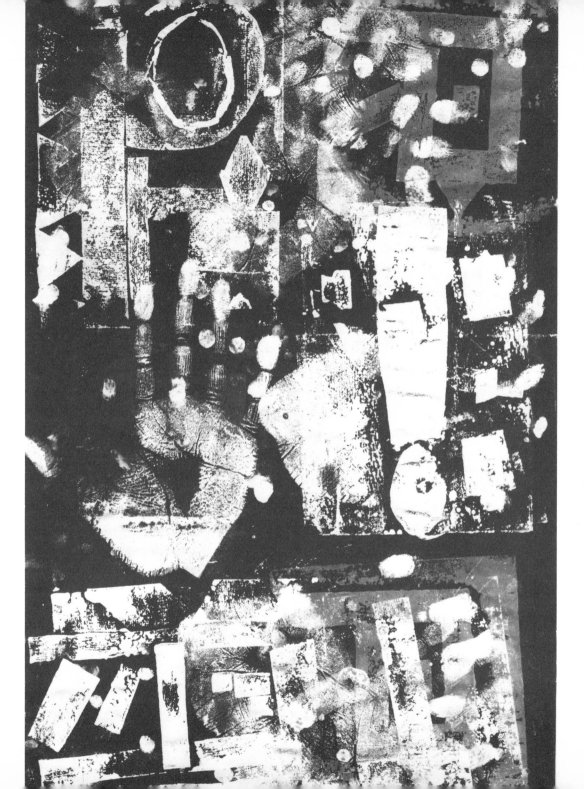

Trees/ Danny age 8/ Printed with the back of a spoon   *. . . using the spoon handle*   *. . . printed on a black piece of paper using colored ink.*

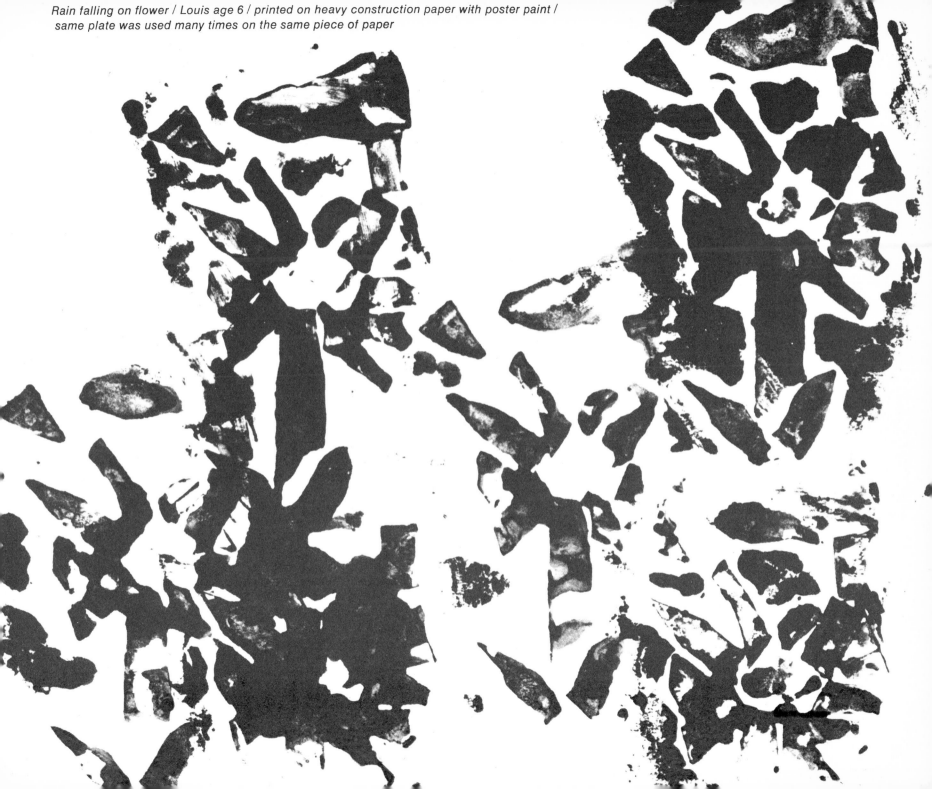

Printing With an Inner Tube

Another easy material you can use to make a printing block is the inner tube of a tire. You can usually get one for nothing at a gasoline station, and one tire will be enough for many printing blocks for you and your friends.

The inner tube is even easier to cut than cardboard. It is more flexible, and it is waterproof. This means that you can use your printing block many more times than you could the cardboard one.

Rubber inner tube plate

Children / Ginny age 5 / rubber inner tube with poster paint on white paper.

49

Painting

Painting is probably what you like best about art. There are many, many colors and varieties of paint. A few people still think that real artists use only oil paints. But since long before oil paints were invented, people have used other kinds of paint, including paints made from soil, from flowers, and from plants. Today, many new kinds of paints have been developed. The paints we are going to talk about in this book are: poster paints, watercolor paints, and plastic paints, or acrylics.

Painting is different from drawing because it is concerned mostly with color. The strokes of a brush are very different from the lines made by a pencil. You will have to practice a bit to get your brush to do what you want it to. But don't worry about making a painting look like something. Just think about the colors, textures, and shapes that you want.

You can say a lot with colors. Think about painting happy colors, sad colors, busy colors, free colors. Think about rain colors and sunshine colors, summer colors and winter colors. And then just paint in any way you feel like.

What You Will Need

There are no rules about how and where to paint. You have probably seen pictures of artists who paint on canvases held up on an easel. If you don't have an easel but like to work standing up, you can tape or tack your paper to a wall, door, or blackboard. You can also work at your desk or on a large table. But don't forget about the floor. This is a very convenient place to work, especially if you are working on large paintings. On the floor you can spread out and have lots of room.

Wherever you work, you should always remember to spread newspapers around you so that you don't splatter paint all over everything. You can also use the newspaper to try out colors when you are mixing paints.

Brushes

You will want to have several different kinds of brushes. You should have thin and fat ones and soft and hard ones. These do not have to be expensive, and they will last a long time if you take good care of them. Never let paint dry on the brush. Some kinds of paint get so hard when they dry that you can never clean them off the brush. When you have finished painting for the day, rinse the brushes under cool running water. Always store brushes standing up in a jar, with the bristles up. If you store them with the bristles down, the bristles will dry out of shape and the brush will be ruined.

But you shouldn't think that you can only

paint with brushes. There are many other tools you can use to give your paintings a different and exciting look. It is probably a long time since you tried to paint with your fingers. Besides making prints with your fingers and hands, you can invent very interesting lines, shapes, and strokes. Try combining finger painting with brush painting. Also experiment with rags dipped in paint, old toothbrushes, sticks, pieces of string, and anything else you can think of.

Paper

You can paint on anything you like. Ever since people discovered paints they have been painting just about everything they could get their hands on, including themselves.

Most often, however, you will be painting on some kind of paper. You can use any kind of paper you want or have around. You can even make very interesting paintings on old newspapers. You should experiment with different kinds of papers and paints. Very hard shiny papers will give different effects from soft absorbent papers. You can paint on cardboard and oak tag, and you can experiment with gluing tissue paper and even paper tissues and newspaper to other paper and painting over this to get different textures. A painting with things glued onto it is called a collage.

Palettes

You usually need to have a special place to put the paint you are using. You should never dip your brush directly into the paint jar, because other colors you are using will get mixed in and you will end up with a lot of jars of mud-colored paint. If you are using a thick kind of paint, you can make a palette. It is easy to make one by cutting out a piece of cardboard about 3 inches wide and 12 inches long. Put some of each color onto this. You can dip your paintbrush into these paints and also mix colors directly on the palette. Throw it away when you have finished. You can make a new one each time you paint.

Of course, you cannot use a palette like this if your paint is thin and runny. Old milk cartons with the tops cut off are very useful for liquid kinds of paint — you can pour a little of each color into each carton.

Water

Milk cartons are also handy for water, and you always need to have a lot of water when you paint. You need it for cleaning your brushes, for thinning paint, and for moistening watercolor paints.

Lion / Kenneth age 8 / poster paint on manila paper

Poster Paints

You probably know what poster paints are because they are the paints most often used in schools. They are inexpensive and easy to use. They usually come in large jars, but they are also available in tubes.

Poster paints come in bright colors. They are opaque, which means that you cannot see through them to the paper underneath. They are very fluid and go onto the paper easily. And they are very quick to dry. They can drip a lot, so remember to cover your work area with newspapers. But don't worry if you do spill some paint — you can clean it up easily with water.

The basic colors you will need are red, yellow, blue, orange, green, purple, black, and white. There are many more colors that you will want to try for special paintings, especially gold and silver and colors that glow. Since poster paints are inexpensive, you can build up a large collection if you take good care of them.

You can make many of your own colors by mixing paints together. The paints will mix better if you thin them with a little water first. You can make orange by mixing red and yellow, green by mixing blue and yellow, and purple by mixing red and blue. Try it and see if the colors you mix yourself are like the ones you buy. You can also make colors lighter by adding white and darker by adding black. You can make the paints very thin by adding water, or you can paint with them just as they are.

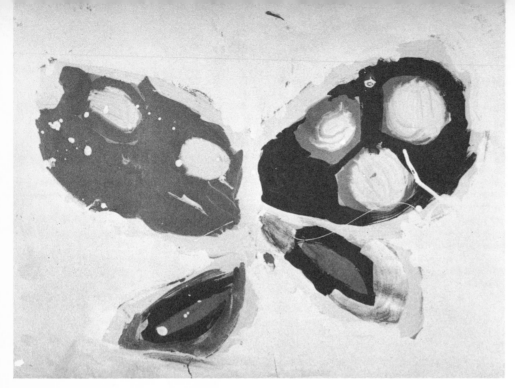

Poster paints work best if you work on large paper with big, bold strokes. A fairly thick brush is better than a thin one. It is best to start by painting simple designs — hearts, circles, diamonds, or even just plain lines in different colors, sizes, and directions. Learn to control the brush and paint and to see how different color combinations look together. Although you can mix the colors while they are wet, see what happens when you paint over a dry color with another color.

You can paint on any kind of paper. Large sheets of brown wrapping paper are very good for making big paintings. Since the colors are opaque, colored paper and newspaper are also very good.

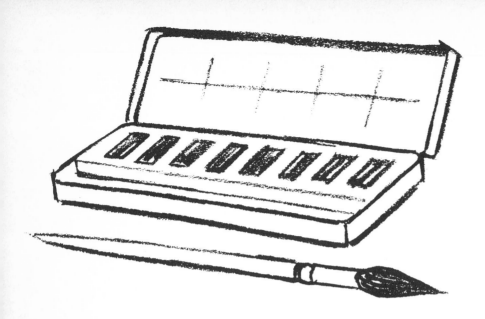

Watercolors

Watercolor paints are quite different from poster paints. Watercolors come in small blocks called cakes. They come in a paint box much like the one shown. There are usually eight colors in a box.

The main difference between watercolor paints and poster paints is that watercolors are transparent, which means you can see through the paint to the paper underneath. To use watercolors you moisten the paint with a wet brush so the color comes off onto the brush. The colors are very light and delicate and you can mix them in the spaces provided in the top of the box.

Watercolor paints are very convenient when you don't have much space. You only need the paints, a jar or milk carton of water to clean your brush, and some paper. This makes watercolors good to use outdoors.

The brushes you use with watercolor paints are smaller and thinner than the ones you usually use with poster paints. You won't need more than one brush for doing watercolor pictures. Watercolor paintings are usually smaller than the ones you do with poster paints, since it is hard to make big ones with a little brush. Usually paper that is 9 by 12 inches is large enough.

Although you can paint with poster paints on almost anything, the kind of paper you use with watercolor makes a great difference in the results you get. If you use a soft paper such as manila, the colors will be very soft and transparent. If you use hard watercolor paper, the colors will be brilliant and much slower to dry.

You can experiment with the colors in your paint box in many different ways. Here are some things you can try:

1. Dampen your paper with a wet brush and apply several colors on it. Notice how the colors spread into each other and how they differ from the colors you get on a dry paper.

2. Go over a yellow with a red, to get an orange. Notice the difference between this kind of orange and the orange you get if you mix your colors before putting them on the paper. Also, notice the difference between both of these and the orange in the paint box.

3. Mix a drop of white in a color. Notice that the paint becomes more opaque as well as lighter. Add more water to a color to brighten it. See the difference between this shade and the shade you get by adding white.

Mix some black with your paints and see what this does to the colors.

A good way to begin painting with watercolors is to divide a piece of paper into several boxes by folding it in half several times. Use each box to experiment with a different color. Divide another piece of paper into boxes and use each box to make simple designs. Make several pictures like this until you have found out all the different ways of using the paints. After that, paint anything you like.

Plastic Paints

The easiest of all paints to use, and perhaps the most fun, are the acrylics, or plastic paints. These are the most modern of all paints. They are like every kind of paint rolled into one. A whole book could be written about the different ways to use them and all the things you can do with them.

What You Will Need

To start with, you will need only these basic colors:

1. White. This is very useful to mix with other colors and you will want a large tube.

2. Black

3. Yellow

4. Red

5. Blue

6. Green

7. Brown

8. Painting medium — glossy. If you mix this with the paint you get a thick, oil-paint effect. When you go over a painting with it, you get a shiny surface. Medium is also a very strong glue.

It is also useful to have a special kind of plastic paint called gesso white. With this you can cover almost every kind of material and make a good surface to paint on. You can also use gesso white to paint out parts of your painting that you want to do over.

With these colors you will be able to get any other color you want by mixing and by adding white or black. If you go to buy plastic paints, you will find that there are many, many varieties of each color, and each of them has a different name. It doesn't matter which one you choose — you can try new ones as you use yours up.

Plastic paints come in tubes and jars. It is important that you use milk cartons and a palette to mix the paints and to thin them. Always keep your brushes moist and rinse them carefully when you are finished. Plastic paints become waterproof when they are dry and your brushes will be ruined if you leave any paint in them.

Here are some of the things you can do with plastic paints:

1. If you use them just as they are, or thinned with just a little water, they will be very much like poster paints. The colors will be bright and opaque.

2. If you mix the paints with a lot of water, they will be like watercolors. The colors will be light and transparent. The one important difference is that when the plastic paint dries, it is waterproof. So you can paint over it without affecting the color below.

3. If you mix the paints with the medium, they will be very shiny.

4. If you use the medium over the painting, you will get a very bright, hard surface that will protect your painting from scratches.

5. You can use plastic paints on almost any surface — paper, cardboard, canvas, wood, masonite, and glass.

6. Because the medium is also a strong glue, you can use it for making collage paintings.

7. You can use gesso white to paint out some parts of your picture and start all over again. You can also use the paints over and over again on top of each other.

You will learn best about these paints if you experiment and use them in every possible way. Here are some projects to get you started:

Paint a layer of gesso white on a piece of cardboard that measures about 12 by 18 inches. Let it dry and cover it with another layer. When this is dry, you will have a very good waterproof surface to paint on.

For your first try with these paints, make a very simple design, perhaps just boxes in various colors. Begin by putting a small amount of paint on your palette. Dip the brush in water and then in the paint and start the design on the cardboard. Notice how smoothly this paint goes on.

Paint in the rest of the design in different colors. Squeeze out only a little bit of paint at a time.

When you have finished, try painting over your picture with the medium. You will see that the colors will get a bright, hard shine. Use the medium to glue things to your painting. Try pieces of paper, scraps of material, feathers, buttons, pieces of stick, sand, or anything you can think of. This makes it more interesting and adds texture.

When you have finished, try painting it all out with gesso white and starting all over again. Use the bumpy textured surface as part of the new design.

Make many pictures using the paints as watercolors, poster paints, and oil paints. Try combining all three in one picture. You will see that the possibilities are endless.

First experiment/ Roger age 12/ Plastic paints on cardboard 12 x 18

Still life/ Linda age 12/ Preliminary sketch/ Plastic Paints on canvas boards

Car/ Linwood age 11/ Plastic paints on cardboard

Football player/ Alfred age 10/ Cardboard store display painted over with plastic paints

Papier Maché

People / Gina Renee & Curtis ages 9 & 10 / Papier-maché figures using basic method described on page 70 then painted with poster paints.

Papier maché can be very messy. But it is also more fun than almost any other art project. You can make sculptures, masks, puppets, and all kinds of strange constructions using papier maché. If you plan your work carefully, you can cut down on the mess.

What You Will Need
Here is what you will need:

1. Wheat paste. (You can find this in any hardware or paint store, but if you can't get it, ordinary baking flour will do.)

2. An empty can or milk carton with the top cut off to mix the wheat paste in.

3. Water

4. Newspapers. You will need plenty of these, because you use a lot of them to protect your work area. You also need them to cut into strips for the papier maché. And you need some to roll into tubes and tie together to make a base on which to paste the strips.

5. The base for papier maché is very important. Besides using rolled up newspapers, you can use blown-up balloons, cardboard tubes from wax paper, bent wire hangers, or anything else that looks right.

6. Tape or string.

7. Paint. You can use poster paints or plastic paints.

How To Make Papier Maché

1. Tear the newspaper into a lot of long strips about 2 inches wide.

2. Mix wheat paste with water — about 1 part paste to 2 parts water.

3. Use some more newspaper to make a base. For example, if you want to make a figure, there are three easy steps. Make a head by crumpling a sheet of newspaper into a ball. Hold it together with tape or tie it with string. Now roll up a few sheets of newspaper into a tube and tape or tie it. Last, put another piece of newspaper over the ball and tie or tape it around the tube to make the neck. You can add arms and legs in the same way.

4. Now dip each strip of newspaper into the paste and then wind it on the base. If you use too much paste, the paper won't stick, so wipe off each piece with your fingers. If the papier maché gets too wet anyway, use some of the newspaper strips dry — they will soak up the extra paste.

5. When you have applied about three layers, stop and let them dry overnight. You can then apply more layers if it is necessary. Three layers of papier maché can be very strong when dry and, if your base is not too large, you may not need any more than this.

6. When your work is completely dry and finished, you can paint it with poster paint or use plastic paint.

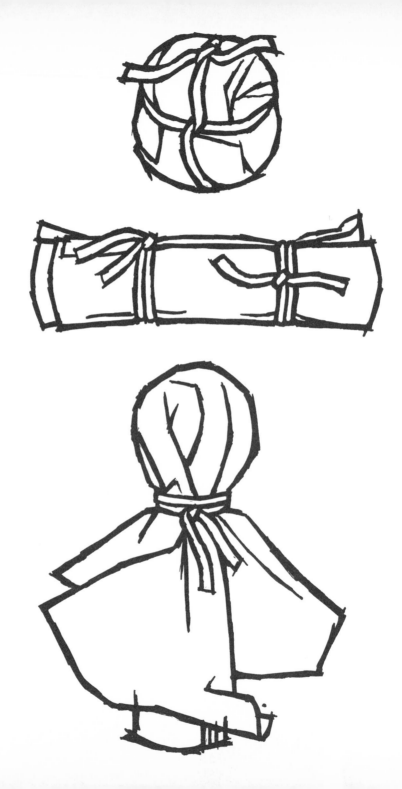

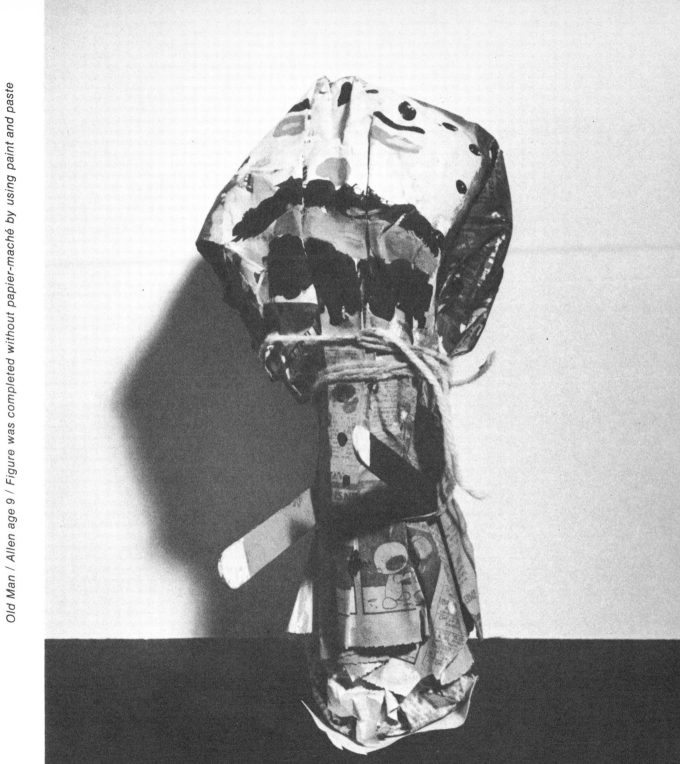

Old Man / Allen age 9 / Figure was completed without papier-maché by using paint and paste

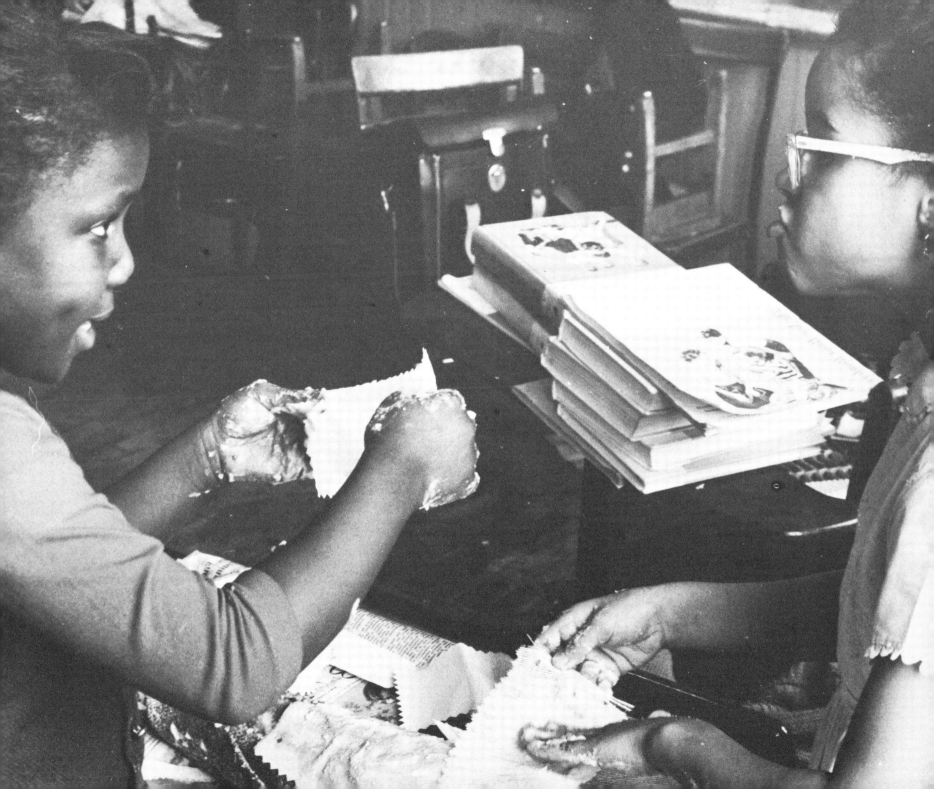

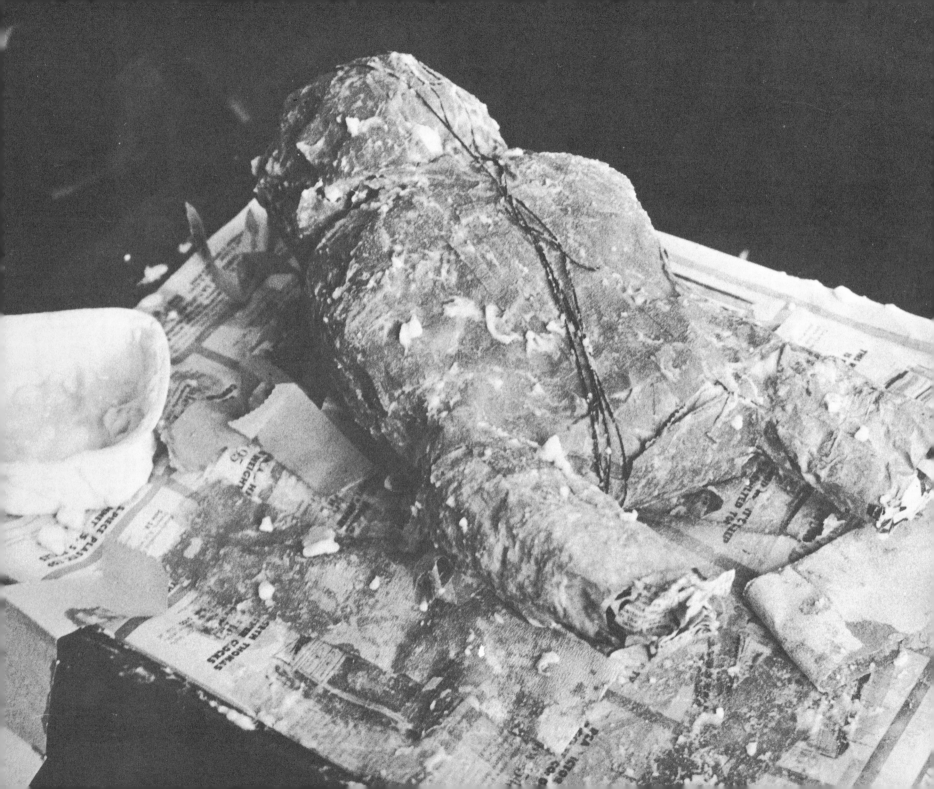

Santa Claus/ Claude age 11/ Paper maché

Two Women / Robin and Jennifer age 10 / Papier-maché using scrap materials

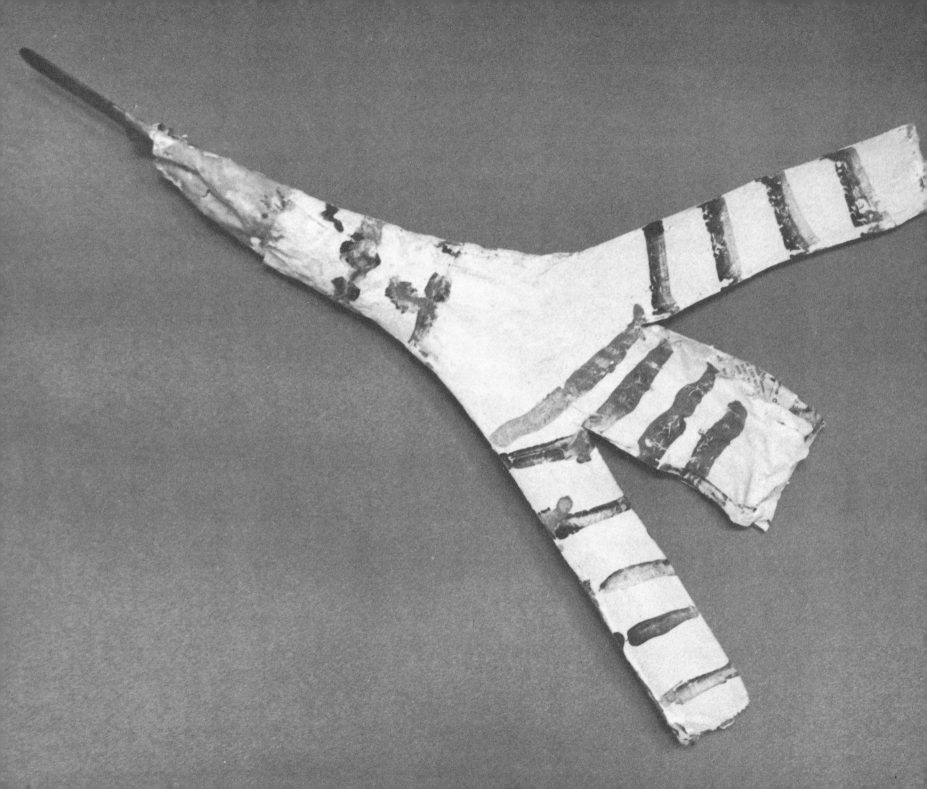

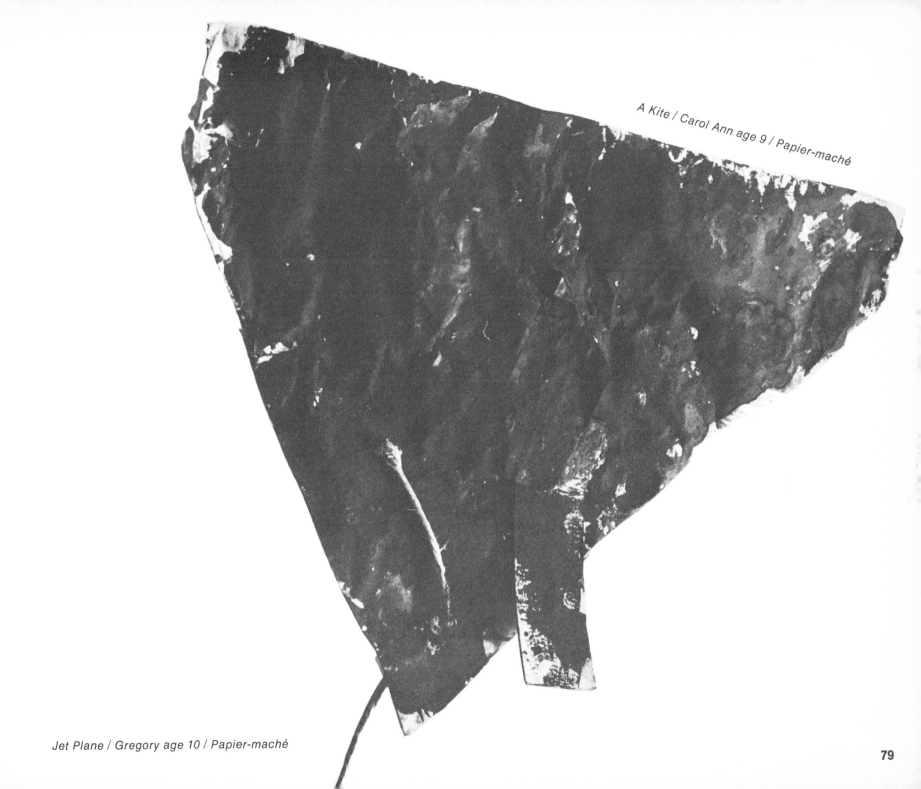

A Kite / Carol Ann age 9 / Papier-maché

Jet Plane / Gregory age 10 / Papier-maché

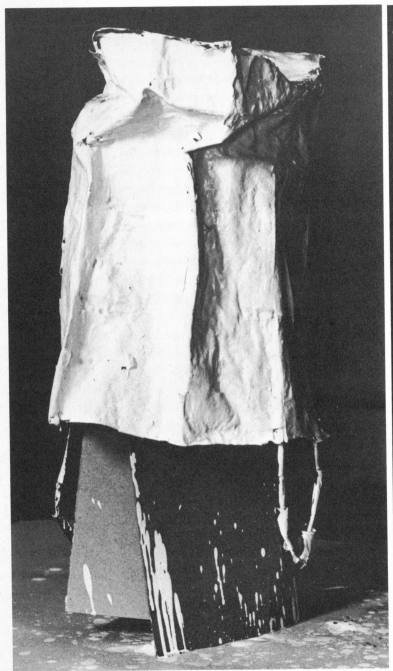
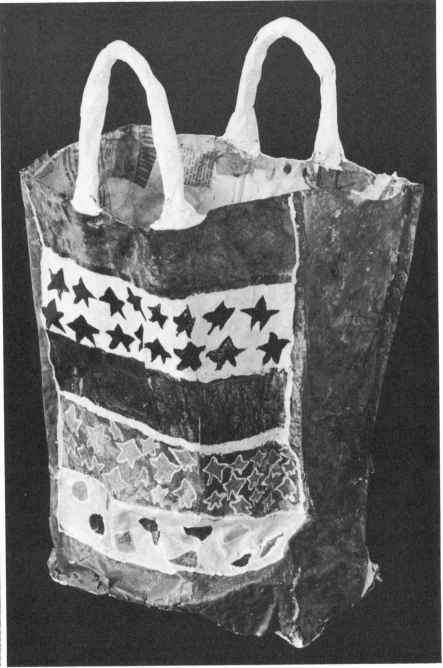

Picture of a comic book hero / Michael age 11 / Papier-maché over a sewing tray

Other Projects To Do With Papier Maché

Papier maché is so strong once it is dry that you can build very complicated structures. Just roll newspapers into tubes of various sizes and tape them so they don't unroll. Then attach them to each other any way you like, using tape or string. If you are going to build a very large structure, it is fun to work with a friend. Apply the newspaper strips. Be careful that they don't get too wet, or your structure will collapse. Let it dry completely after every three layers of papier maché. When it is completed and dry, paint it in the most exciting way you can imagine.

Another thing to do with papier maché is to cover different objects with it. It is fun to use the most unlikely things: an old hat, old shoes, gloves, cups, spoons, saucers, pillows, and anything else you can think of. Just make whatever you choose be the base and cover it with several layers of papier maché. Let it dry and decorate it with paint.

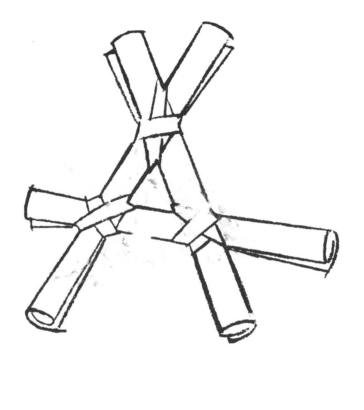

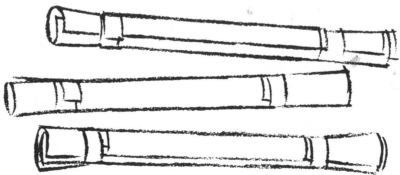

Tubular sculpture / Kenneth and Marle age 11 / Papier-maché

Plaster Tiles

The very simplest materials can be used to make very beautiful things. We mostly think of plaster as the material walls are made of, but making sculpture in plaster is a very old art. A project that is fun and easy is making tiles with plaster.

What You Will Need

The only materials you need are plaster of Paris and Plasticine (or some other kind of modeling clay). Both are very inexpensive and easy to get. Plaster is used to make walls in most buildings, and if you have seen walls being plastered, you know how smoothly and beautifully it can be worked.

Plasticine is a material like clay that doesn't get hard. It is often used in schools to do modeling. Since it doesn't harden, it can be used over and over again.

How To Make Plaster Tiles

1. To make plaster tiles, you first have to make a mold. Smooth out the Plasticine on a piece of cardboard — use your fingers or a rolling pin. Make a slab about half an inch thick and 6 inches square, and cut or press a design into it. Anything can be used to make the design — a pencil, spoon, fork, comb, or even your finger. If letters are part of your design, remember to make them backwards, just as if you were making a printing block. You can change the design as much as you like by just smoothing the Plasticine out and beginning again.

2. After you have finished the design, make a wall around the Plasticine. This is to hold the liquid plaster you will pour in. If you have enough Plasticine, you can build the wall out of it. If you don't have enough, you can use cardboard and seal the wall at each corner with some of the Plasticine.

3. Now mix the plaster of Paris. There are directions on the bag to make a perfect mixture. Use an old tin can or empty milk carton with the top cut off to mix the plaster in, and make only a small amount. You will need very little for most pieces, and you can always mix more. When the plaster of Paris is smoothly mixed, pour it into the mold and let it dry completely. The drying time will depend on how thin or thick the plaster is, but it usually takes only a couple of hours.

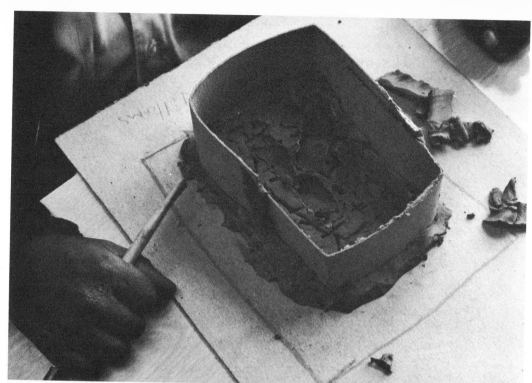

4. When the plaster is completely dry, you are ready to remove the tile from the mold. First peel off the walls. Some of the cardboard might stick to the plaster but this gives an interesting surface to paint on, so you can leave it on. Now lift the plaster away from the Plasticine. The Plasticine won't stick to the plaster and should come away easily. Save it to use again. The plaster tile now has a relief — a raised and reversed version of your design in the Plasticine.

The plaster tiles look very nice when they are hung on the wall. You can do this by taping a piece of string to the back. Or you can insert a paper clip into the plaster when it is still wet, leaving enough of the clip sticking out to hang on a hook.

A tulip / Barbara age 11 / Plaster tile unpainted

5. Plaster tiles look nice left unpainted, but you can make them even more beautiful if you paint them. The best kind of paint to use for this is plastic paint. If you mix medium with the paint it will dry with a shiny glaze. This will also make the tile waterproof. If you use poster paint or plastic paint thinned with water, the tiles will have a soft dull look which is also very beautiful.

Designs / Morris age 11 / Plaster tiles unpainted

Baseball player / John age 9 / Plaster tile

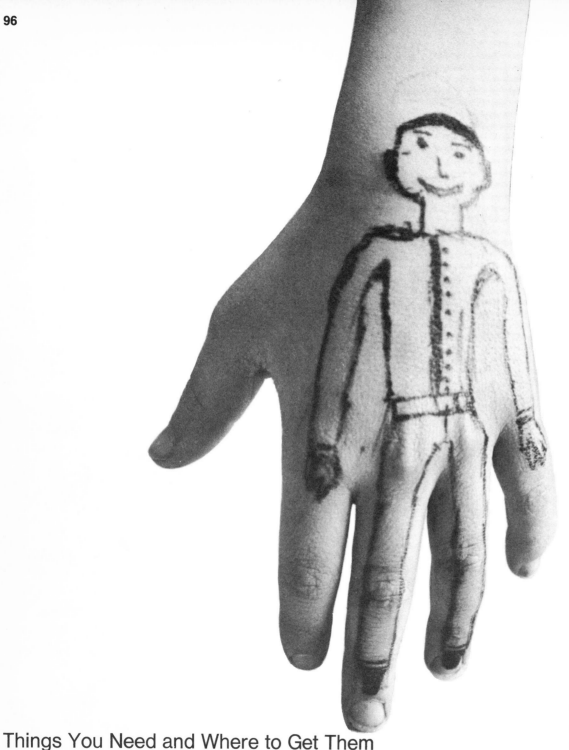

Listed below are some of the basic materials mentioned in this book which you will need for drawing, printing, painting, making sculpture and papier maché. Of course, there are many other things which you can use, and the more materials you try out, the more exciting your results will be.

Crayons
Colored Chalks (Pastels)
Charcoal
Charcoal Fixative
Felt-tipped Pens
Printing Ink
Rubber Printing Rollers (Brayers)
Poster Paints
Watercolors
Plastic Paints (Acrylics or Polymers)
Cardboard
Oak Tag
Tissue Paper
Brown Wrapping Paper
Colored Paper
Manila Paper
Newspaper
Paintbrushes
Plaster of Paris
Plasticine (Modeling Clay)
Wheat Paste

Most of these supplies can be found at five-and-ten-cent stores, and some you will already have them at home. Other good places to buy them are stationery stores and art-supply stores. Hardware stores carry plaster of Paris, Plasticine, and wheat paste.

Things You Need and Where to Get Them